THE TAO OF THE 21st CENTURY

The wisdom of the Tao in modern words

Karsten Ramser

Many people know that the drop merges
in the ocean

but few know that the ocean merges in
the drop.

Kabir.

KARSTEN RAMSER

Title: The Tao of the 21st century
Author: Karsten Ramser
Cover: Mike Feelright
Copyright 2018 by Karsten Ramser and Maribel Rosado Escribano
Copyright 2018 by A.R.T. EDITION
Avda. Constitución 46
03769 Sanet y Negrals, Alicante.
Spain.
Published by Karsten Ramser at Smashwords
www.karstenramser.net
info@karstenramser.net

For Michael, my little brother.

3

Introduction

The Tao Te Ching has an essence that is beyond time, but the words are not timeless, they are depending on the Zeitgeist (the spirit of time).

My intention is to express this essence in modern words.

Like the original text, this book works with aphorisms or sutras. They are an invitation to reflect, not only with the mind, even more important is to contemplate the sutras, to feel them and to let them do the work for you. It is always better to stop reading and start feeling.

The aphorisms are the direct expression of the essence of the Tao. When you allow them to empty your mind and fill your heart transformation will happen naturally without any effort.

The Tao Te Ching in itself leads toward the transpersonal reality.

This book is one more drop in the ocean of consciousness written in the knowledge that nothing and nobody can stop the conscious evolution.

I wish you a good journey.
Karsten Ramser.

The Tao

The Tao is the essence of everything that exists.

Life itself is born out of the Tao;

it was before the beginning of time and space.

Nothing exists without it.

It is the Oneness in all forms of life.

The eternal flow of existence.

All individual lifeforms are notes in the symphony of the Tao.

The Tao is beyond all description. We call it the Tao because the mind needs words to understand and through the mind we are conscious. We also could call it the Un-namable or the Self, but it really doesn't matter how we name it; what counts is the experience.

Our job is to realise consciously the Tao.

The word Tao means in Chinese the way or the path. Around this path grows the knowledge of the Tao, it helps us to become the experience of our innermost nature in alignment with the essence of everything.

The knowledge of the Tao is not a teaching, philosophy nor a spiritual tradition. It is the map that indicates the way - and that's it.

The Tao of the 21st century
The wisdom of the Tao in modern words

0

There exists something before everything.
Something before God or the big bang.
Before time and space.
Empty and eternally present.
Right now, it is in us, in you, in me,
in the stars, stones, plants and animals,
in absolutely everything.
No words can describe it
and for lack of a better word,
we call it the Tao.

1

The experience of the Tao has no name.
It can't be investigated, nor can it be trained.
Beyond all words, names and concepts,
it can be experienced.
Living the experience of the Tao
is Selfknowledge without the delusion of I do.
Experience and realisation are one.
It is the pathless path in the eternal now
for the benefit of all existence.
Free of attachment
the manifestations of the Tao can be known.
Wishful thinking and attached feelings
without Selfknowledge
leads to egoism and insanity.
The Tao can be experienced perfectly
without any knowledge,
but the words make it possible
for us to be conscious about the Tao.
The appropriate interpretation of the Tao leads to
beauty, understanding and compassion.
The inappropriate interpretation leads to
egoism, confusion and suffering.
Experience and knowledge are real,
both emanate from the Tao.
The experience is simple,
the knowledge is complex.
By using the appropriate means
we extend personal existence
beyond the limitations
of the complexity of the mind,
in this way experience and knowledge merge.

2

Like the mirror can't see itself.
It's impossible to know the Tao itself.
In contemplation the Tao
can be conscious about itself.
The Tao is One and it splits in two,
out of that duality the world arises.
Duality is comparison and differentiation,
through them, reality is known.
We see beauty because we know the ugly.
There is no good without the bad.
Without the short there is no long.
We can lose only what we have.
Death exists because there is life.
We suffer for the attachment
to one part of the duality.
We want the impossible;
happiness without pain
success without failure
health without disease
living without death.
The right understanding,
which arises from the experience of the Tao,
is freedom from attachment to duality.
Comparison and differentiation
might still be used for practical reasons,
judgement is needed.
The flow of the Tao happens,
without any need for force or control,
when we accept both parts of duality.
In this flow, we act without doing,
we teach without speech.

Things come and go, we have but we don't own;
we never know what leads to what.
Be still, rest in the Tao and let it flow.

3

In humility we find wisdom and beauty.
The everyday living
and the little things teach us humility.
When we try to be somebody
we are nobody.
The Tao is what it is,
perfect, spontaneous and humble.
Emptying your mind of wishful thinking
means to be humble.
A humble heart is fulfilled.
It doesn't need more than it has.
Possessions come and go,
some are great, some are small,
whoever searches for possessions
will never have enough.
By being humble and flexible
the energy is at its perfect state.
Minimise your attachment
and do not train yourself
in false and empty speech.
Nothing to prove nor to convince.
In humility we serve for the good of existence.
Behind all the masks, names, status and titles,
we see reality as it is.

4

The Tao has no beginning nor end.
Its nature is the constant flow.
Never exhausted nor overfilled.
It's the eternal void, full of everything possible.
It never loses its infinite generosity
and nourishes all existence.
Nothing can destroy it.
The Tao brings all resistance down.
His nature is like water.
Who lives in the knowledge of the Tao
is like water too.
Recognising our timeless nature
we can act in consequence
seeing the unity of everything in everybody.
The experience of the Tao can't be transmitted
as it is always present.

5

The nature of the Tao is emptiness.
Out of this emptiness arises duality.
Good and bad, black and white, heaven and earth.
That's the world we know.
Everything is in constant change.
What is good today can be bad tomorrow,
what you love today, you may not love tomorrow.
Only what is empty can be filled.
Stay in emptiness and you truly will be fulfilled.
Actions rise out of the Tao,
with no intention,
nor a centre or a final goal.
When you act in this way,
you find kindness and compassion in your heart.
Your doing is spontaneous and free of attachment.
Emptiness is the non-dual experience of the Tao.

6

Like a mountain lake,
a contemplative mind is
still, calm and transparent.
Act when it's needed.
The action happens naturally.
Out of stillness and energy
rise the world of form and action.
Both are ever-present in all existence.
The contemplative mind is non-dual,
there is no judgement,
no comparison nor differentiation.
Contemplation is the gateway
to the oneness of existence.
In this awareness we are one.

7

The Tao is beyond time,
never born,
thus it can never die.
Beyond space,
infinite and empty,
thus ever-present in all existence.
Who lives consciously in the Tao
has no need to search for it.
All knowledge that we can achieve is
selective and dual,
born out of the sense perception
and the thinking mind.
Realising this, is detachment from duality.
See the world as One,
all objects are seen as One,
all beings seen as One.
When you see everything as One,
you see the Tao,
empty of inherent existence,
infinite and eternal.

8

Water nourishes the world.
Without water there will be no world.
Be like water,
flowing in the here and now,
always flexible.
Water never controls; it flows.
When it gets stuck,
it waits patiently for the right moment,
knowing that this moment will come.
Water is humble and powerful,
it does what it does,
flows without intention,
it has no need to get anywhere
so it goes everywhere.
When we understand the nature of water,
we understand ourselves,
this is the knowledge of the Tao.
In this knowledge
there is no need for wishful thinking,
no need to search for a better future
nor to get stuck in the past
and so we are free of inner conflict.
No inner conflict,
no conflict in the world.

9

Duality always has two sides
which are in natural balance.
Living in extremes creates imbalance.
Walking the middle path,
we don't need to fill the cup to the brim
nor desire more than we need,
searching happiness inwardly
and not in the external world.
Desiring too many things troubles inner peace,
being attached to them is like
being hungry after eating;
being thirsty after drinking,
or finding fulfillment - and still it's not enough.
In the middle path,
you don't need titles to know who you are.
Naturally you do good,
because you see the basic goodness
in all existence.
Do what you have to do quietly,
do it in natural ease,
no need to force,
no need to control.
When all is done,
step back and feel the serenity.
This is the middle path and the nature of the Tao.

10

Mind is thought and thought is mind.
Mind without the knowledge of the Tao
is like a never cleaned mirror.
The vision is confused and unclear.
We can't see our real face.
From this moment on we start searching.
That's the wandering mind.
The wandering mind is never still,
living in constant distraction and separation.
All it needs is nothing, thinking for thinking.
There is no peace
when you are attached to the wandering mind.
Be aware of the rushing
from one thought to another.
Do not resist nor try to stop it.
Let it go.
Contemplate without judgement.
Reflect without intention.
Cultivate without the need to possess.
Be open to the constant change.
Act free from the outcome.
Love without interfering.
See the Oneness in everything.
That is detachment from the wandering mind.

11

Only the cup that is empty can be filled.
Only a mind that is empty
can learn the knowledge of the Tao.
All that exists is empty.
Nothing has an inherent
and independent existence.
All is interrelated;
patterns in patterns in patterns towards infinity.
It is the emptiness that moves the world,
without it, there will be no existence at all.
When you look for meaning in life,
you can find it in the emptiness.

12

Thanks to the light we see the world,
too much light makes us blind.
Music is the gateway
to the mysterious feeling of being alive.
Too much music makes us deaf.
Knowledge gives us understanding.
Too much knowledge creates confusion.
In the hunting for pleasure
we are losing contact with the earth.
By collecting things,
we are losing the connection to ourselves.
Contemplate the world and trust the inner voice.

13

It's common sense
to seek success and avoid failure,
to love life and fear death
and to identify with the ego.
When we understand the path of the Tao,
we don't worry about these things.
It's common sense
that the "I" is the centre of the universe.
The Tao has no centre, thus the universe has none.
Living a simple and quiet life,
we see the oneness in a drop of water
and feel it in one single breath.
In this humility we love the world,
remaining inwardly unmoved
about what happens externally.

14

When you name it, it's gone.
When you touch it, it has vanished already.
It doesn't make a sound,
but there will no music without it.
It is the formless in the form.
The faceless in every face.
It is the light in the darkness
and the darkness in the light.
Beyond all understanding,
the closest we can say is, emptiness.

15
The knowledge of the Tao, is like a tree;
it grows.
The knowledge of the Tao,
is like a river;
it merges into the ocean.
It is not a question of what we do
in order to achieve this knowledge.
There is no specific standard or rule.
What counts is the experience itself.
The trust in your own experience is the ground
on which the knowledge of the Tao grows.
Everyone can have the experience,
but this doesn't provide the knowledge.
Even when words can't explain the Tao,
they can give an interpretation
that is in harmony with the experience.
We can't force the experience of the Tao
but we can learn the knowledge
and this opens up widely the possibilities
for the experience of the Tao.

16
Being one with the Tao is being at home.
Detach yourself from the concept of "I do",
understand the concept of "it happens".
Life happens.
Everything happens at once in the here and now,
multidimensional, beyond time and space.
Understanding this, is serenity.
Not understanding this, is insanity.
Knowing the eternal nature of the Tao
means to be open to constant change.

17

When we are healthy
we do not pay attention to the body
but when we get sick it requires our full attention.
In the same way,
when the Tao flows we don't pay attention to it
and when not, it requires all our attention.
When we are happy
we don't ask why and how
but when we suffer
we search for the why and the how.
Suffering appears when we have lost
the flow of the Tao.
If we could trust in the flow while we suffer
what will happen?
In the understanding
that suffering is the first step
to realising the Tao
lies the secret of transformation.

18

To forget that all existence is the Tao
gives rise to ethics and good works,
instead of being in the flow
we try to be wise and good.
Trust is replaced by control.
Control leads to imbalance.
Imbalance leads to suffering
and suffering finally leads again to the Tao.

19

The wish to be better than we are
makes us slaves of the mind and time.
Thinking there will be a better future
is the negation of the here and now.
Negating the present moment
is negating life itself.
Leave wisdom and holiness behind
and come back to the simplicity of the breath.
We don't have to do good works
when we are rooted in the Tao.
Why search for a new consciousness,
when we are already conscious?
Let the natural flow
wash away the wishful thinking of the ego
and the beauty of existence
will unfold spontaneously.
By being one with life,
we see that life is the wonder in itself.
The arrogant wish to make it better,
brings for every new achievement new problems.
Real progress arises out of natural serenity
and not out of wishful thinking.
Only the heart that is at peace
and the contemplative mind
are able to understand the structure of reality,
which is the very foundation
of conscious evolution.

20

The extraordinary flows naturally
when we stop identifying with thought.
When thoughts are just like waves in the ocean,
the Tao takes over.
When this happens life becomes
an expression of the Tao,
the ordinary becomes extraordinary.
The Tao is everywhere:
having a cup of tea; going to the mountain;
acquiring titles or being simply a street sweeper.
To live in the presence of the Tao,
is the greatest experience of all.
In the understanding of the Tao
our hearts are full
and our minds understand emptiness.
This way, we see the miracle in existence.
Everybody knows that the drop
merges into the ocean,
but very few know that the ocean
merges into the drop.
Many search for the extraordinary
but very few find it in the ordinary.

21
Be aware of the Tao,
without wishful thinking
and emotional demands,
the flow becomes the natural state.
Leave concepts behind.
There is no need to explain nor describe.
Before everything the Tao is the Tao.
Beyond existence and non-existence
is the Tao.
Stop searching for it
and it will find you.
Look inside and see.

22

Fulfilment rises out of emptiness.
If you want to live you have to die.
Without the light there will be no darkness,
and because of the darkness you can see the light.
Accept life as it is
and there will be integrity.
The person who is whole has no need to shine;
the light within shines.
When there is nothing to prove,
trust is found.

23

Trust and live life completely.
We have forgotten the essence of life.
Find the essence in reality as it is -
and the searching will end.
In the loss you will find yourself.
Don't get stuck in the known,
let the unknown find you.
Be still -
and life will be a dance.
Die in this life -
and you will live eternally.
Open yourself to the Tao
and it will happen.

24

Balance is the nature of the Tao.
Living in balance is living in the Tao.
We are what we are,
don't try to be somebody else.
If you live in your dream world
of how life "should" be, you suffer.
All that is not balanced will vanish.
Extremes lead to imbalance.
Imbalance is the insanity of the egocentric world.
First of all stay in balance.
Balance is the playground of nature.
Do what you have to do and let it go,
the Tao will do the rest.

25

The self-organising, creative principle
is the most basic and the most elevated tendency.
It moves the world.
It is the Tao in action.
Understanding this principle we realise
the organic, living structure-pattern of the universe.
Laws and rules are inventions of the mind.
What moves the world is not fixed in laws and rules,
but flexible patterns and the infinite ocean of possibility.
Respecting these patterns
and being open to the possibilities,
reveals the human potential
which is not different from the potential of the Tao.

26

The path of the Tao is the natural flow of existence.
No matter what you do or where you are,
no matter what you feel or think,
the Tao is always your true nature.
Focus your attention on this.
You are never separated from the Tao.
Be aware of the beauty of existence,
contemplate the thinking mind,
stay in the simplicity and be humble.
This is the guide to remember who you are.
Don't force it,
just do it.
When you can't,
go back to the stillness
and learn from the breath.

27

Being here and now is the natural way.
The Tao has no plan,
it is doing without doing.
It is the unnamable intelligence
that pushes us forward.
All great discoveries, inventions and artworks
are made by mistakes, errors and intuition.
It is always the unknown that reveals
the next step in evolution.
Following the Tao
is the journey into the unknown.

28

Talking embodies silence.
Creativity embodies receptivity.
Living embodies death.
When considering any form, thing or being,
have in mind its opposite.
To understand the world,
you have to know both sides.
To understand yourself,
you have to be both sides.
When you find fulfilment in the heart,
you also find it in the world.

29
Life is what it is.
Why do you pretend to change it?
Before you can change something
you have to understand it.
Do you think you understand life?
Do you know what leads to what?
Real change happens out of emptiness.
Peace and stillness are the base of action.
Are you empty, still and at peace?
Do you really believe that the one who is serene
has the need to tell the world what to do?
When you understand the meaning
of doing without doing,
then you understand
that the wish to change the world
is the very reason why we destroy it.
When you are one with the Tao
then change happens naturally.
Step back.
Observe that the need for control
leads to conflict and imbalance.
Live the life.
Follow the inner voice.
Live it completely and with passion.
Let the power of the Tao find its way.

30
Forcing something or somebody
is hard, inflexible, dogmatic and creates resistance.
The Tao is soft, flexible, open and gentle.
Using force, creates more resistance;
it's a vicious circle.
Even when it is used with good intention,
it will always turn against you.
This is the lesson of history.
Not living in the knowledge of the Tao
implies the misunderstanding that life is ours:
our life, our country, our planet....
When we believe this,
we believe we have the right,
even the (divine) obligation, to manipulate
by force and violence.
This is fighting life.
Living in harmony
the need to control disappears.
This knowledge is 1000 times stronger
than all belief systems, dogmas,
philosophies and ideals.
By being in harmony with yourself,
you are in harmony with life.

31

Being at peace is the nature of the Tao,
it's our nature.
In the absence of peace fear arises.
Fear is to forget who you are;
it's the separation from the flow of life.
When we are driven by fear,
there is no joy even in the midst of beauty.
Violence is the tool of fear.
If we live in harmony
there is no fear,
therefore, there is no need for violence.
Give up. Let it go.
Accept your eternal being.
Understanding that you are the Tao
is the end of fear.

32
The Tao is smaller than nothing
and bigger than everything.
It is incomprehensible.
Emptiness is the gateway to the Tao.
Stay in the awareness of the Tao
and all will be in perfect harmony.
The earth will be the most amazing beautiful place.
People will live in peace
and all needs will be satisfied.
Institutions, governments
and religions will vanish naturally.
The self-organising, creative principle
will take over.
Humans will merge into the Tao consciously,
like the rivers merge into the ocean.
This is not a dream. It is the reality of the Tao.

33

There is knowledge of the ego -
and the belief that it is the centre.
There is the knowledge of the world -
which may be seen as intelligence.
There is the knowledge of oneself -
which is wisdom.
There is the knowledge of the Tao -
which transcends all other knowledge.
Knowledge is selective and relative,
there is no final truth
beyond the here and now.

34

All existence is the Tao
flowing naturally without intention.
Everything is born out of the Tao,
yet it doesn't create.
Creation is a myth of the mind.
The mind can't understand
that life is one unique event
in the eternal present.
It can think only in linear form,
reducing existence to a story
with a beginning and an end.
It has no answer to the important questions,
nor can it provide peace.

35

There are many beautiful things in the world
and it's perfectly fine to enjoy them.
There is a lot of suffering in the world
and when we learn from it, it makes sense.
The Tao welcomes everything:
beauty, pain, suffering, joy,
anger, conflict, compassion;
everything has its place.
Even in the midst of the worst suffering,
the Tao is present.
If you stay focused on the presence of the Tao
you will find peace in your heart.
It's the most beautiful transformation.

36

It is the nature of nature
that all forms and all beings
are constantly changing.
It's the timeless river of existence.
What lives dies
and death becomes life.
Every state of being will pass.
Nothing stands still.
We can't change this.
In this coming and going
the Tao remains.

37

Nature has no plan,
everything happens spontaneously.
Everything gets done naturally.
Life has no reason,
it happens because it happens.
Contemplate life without judging.
Observe nature,
let her be your teacher.
Practice the art of non-doing.
Live unattached to the results,
this is the Tao in action.

38

There is nothing more powerful than the Tao.
Wanting power is a sign of fear.
Fear and power
lead to conflict without solution.
The tool of fear and power is control.
The illusion of controlling leads to stagnation
and stagnation is the end of life.
We can only go with life, not against it.
Let the self-organising, creative principle take over;
when you can act in harmony with it, act.
When not, be still and rest.
A truly powerful person
acts without attachment
and leaves nothing undone.
Acting with attachment is endless work.

39

When the Tao lives in the heart of the people
the world is in harmony.
The earth, the sky and all living beings are One.
In this harmony we see reality as it is.
When we forget the Tao
harmony is broken.
We declare the world ours
and separate the unity of existence into pieces
that we pretend to own.
Nature becomes a shopping mall
and insanity becomes the norm.
Earth, air and water are poisoned
and animals become extinct.
Living without the Tao
is a rat-race that never ends,
always wishing for more than we have.
Rushing from one moment to another
in the hope that the future will bring
what is now apparently missing.
Searching for greatness and salvation,
we believe that we can save the world.
Saving the world!
But from whom or what?
Once forget the place where we belong,
we declare ourselves the centre of the world.
Humility is the foundation of greatness.
A truly great person will never claim to be great;
he or she lives in serenity,
detached from the outcome of action.

40

Nature is constant flow, never stopping.
She never asks for anything in return.
She returns everything to the source.
Life and death are one.
Being and non-being are one.
You, I, we and the Tao are one.
Returning to the Tao consciously is the way.

41

First when we hear of the Tao,
we laugh about it,
then we doubt it,
then we believe it,
later we practice it
and finally we embody it.
That's the natural way to realise the Tao.
There is time for everything:
time to be born,
time to play and grow,
time for pain, confusion and suffering,
time for understanding and misunderstanding,
and time to die.
In all these times the Tao is present,
it nourishes everything,
only the Tao completes all things.

42

Out of the Tao rises
I Amness,
out of I Amness rises duality;
duality gives birth to all existence.
Don't try to understand it, you can't.
Relax and learn the great lesson of not knowing.
Not knowing
brings harmony.
Not knowing is not ignorance
it is to know your degree of ignorance
and this opens your heart and mind.
In the experience of the non-knowing
your search has an end.

43

The soft overcomes the hard.
The good overcomes the bad.
The liquid overcomes the solid.
Light overcomes darkness.
That is the natural way.
This knowledge
can be transmitted without words.
Action can take place without doing.
That is the way of the Tao.

44

Don't get confused,
money is not wealth,
stillness is not the absence of sound,
success is not happiness
and peace is not the absence of violence.
If you look for fulfilment in books,
in the holy scripts,
in religion, in ideals, or by following others
you truly will never be fulfilled.
The here and now gives you everything you need.
There was never anything missing
life is perfect as it is.

45
Life seems to be one thing
and then turns out to be something different:
Love becomes hate;
good intention becomes the road to destruction;
the fool becomes wise.
We never know what leads to what.
Taking the appearance of the world
for a solid and definite reality
is the shortcut
to suffering, disharmony and imbalance.
Nothing has an inherent
and independent existence.
Look beyond the appearance and see reality.

46

In contemplation we see perfection;
we even see that imperfection has its function.
Being in harmony with the Tao
provides progress, wealth and respect.
Not being in harmony with the Tao
leads to stagnation, destruction and fear.
Believing that we are separated and independent beings
is the greatest illusion.
Out of it rises (the mental) fear
that makes the Tao invisible.
That's the worst thing that can ever happen.
In the knowledge of the Tao all fear will vanish.

47

The less you know, the more you talk.
The more you know, the less you understand.
To open your heart to the world
means to know less.
Be comfortable in the non-knowing.
If you want to see the essence of the Tao
observe the space between the things
and not the things themselves.
Space leads to stillness,
stillness leads to emptiness.
Emptiness is the essence of the Tao.
In emptiness we do without doing,
we see without looking,
we travel without leaving,
we are without being.
In emptiness we are the Tao.

48

Knowledge is the way of understanding
but it can never be the experience.
Knowledge represents the world
but it will never be the world.
One thing is to know the pathless path of the Tao
but it is something completely different to walk it.
Knowledge adds.
The Tao removes.
Knowledge is practical.
The Tao is essential.

49

The Tao is the essential goodness of life.
Living in the Tao means
to see the goodness in all.
It is the understanding that the good and the bad
are in essence one.
Living in this goodness
trust rises naturally in the heart.
This trust erases false concepts
and ideas from the mind.
A free mind is capable of seeing the Tao
in everything and everybody.

50
Living in the Tao
reveals our impersonal and eternal nature.
Whatever takes place -
it's not personal.
The body-mind-complex (the "I") will die,
but we have nothing to lose anymore.
All illusions are gone
we just change the form.
Knowing our true nature
is the end of an independent "I".
Death is in this knowledge like
going to bed after a good day's work.

51

Everything is an expression of the Tao,
interrelated and guided
by the self-organising, creative principle.
The whole existence is I Amness,
perfect and free,
impersonal and eternal.
This one single moment,
the here and now,
is the love of the Tao.

52

The love of the Tao is the natural flow of existence.
Whoever is at one with it,
is at one with all.
This is freedom from fear and death.
Not understanding this
reduces us to be a separate and independent dot
in the universe,
fighting life in the hope for peace.
That's the madness of common sense.
A free mind is free of attachment.
It's the attachment that causes the trouble.
Accept that you are the Tao now
in a form of a human being.
In this acceptance you return to The Source.
This is the practice of eternity.

53
Life is easy,
the mind makes it complicated.
Use the mind and don't let it use you;
serenity is found.
Without the balance of serenity
rich people declare themselves poor,
governments work for themselves
and not for the people,
the egocentric mind
replaces compassion and kindness.
The world becomes a shopping mall.
To forget the Tao is insanity.
To be centred in the Tao is harmony.

54

When the Tao is deeply rooted in oneself
nothing and nobody can take it away.
But when you try to hold it,
it's like smoke in the air.
The quality of the Tao is real
if it grows from inside to outside.
It nourishes the body, the heart and the mind.
When the mind is clear and the heart is calm,
it benefits the whole universe.

55
The one who flows with the Tao,
has the nature of water.
Water is in harmony with the environment,
it has no need to change anything
and that's why it changes everything.
It is soft and gentle
but if needed
it takes mountains away or cuts steel.
Water is patient, consistent and unstoppable.
Let water be your teacher.
Flow like water.
Let things come and let things go.
In this consciousness you never grow old
you see the world with the eyes of a young mind.

56

Who hurries, misses the moment.
Who boasts, misses serenity.
Who pretends to know,
knows very little or nothing.
Stay quiet and speak only
when you have something to say.
Do not demand that life owes you something
nor demand that people respect you.
When you know who you are,
you are free of the opinions of others.
There is no need to shine when the light is bright.
Come back to simplicity.
In simplicity the complications of life will
settle down just like that.
All you have to do is
be patient and still.
That's the natural way.
In simplicity
you don't have to be concerned to make friends
nor to avoid enemies.
Glory or harm, praise or blame,
loved or not being loved,
all these things are like leaves in the wind,
but you are like the tree,
simple, flexible and humble.

57

You can't own life.
When you accept that you own nothing,
you will have more than enough.
Stop trying to get and to have,
just do it and be who you are.
Remember the practice of eternity
and peace will be your reality.
Know yourself
and the flow of life will guide you.
Detach yourself
and the amazing beauty will be visible.

58

Gentleness is the light on the path.
But, at times, the Tao is dark and heavy,
although its nature is light and joyful.
When we take it too seriously,
repression and depression arise.
We can't walk the path by force.
High ideals make us blind.
We can't make people happy;
the very intent to interfere, leads surely to misery.
Trusting the Tao is trusting life itself.
Maybe we don't see or understand it;
but this trust is the practice.

59

Living in serenity requires moderation.
Being detached from your thoughts and actions.
Let go of your own importance.
See the bigger picture.
Be tolerant like the sky,
flexible like the bamboo
and act in consequence.
In this moderation you see
what happens as it happens,
without your stories.
This is the most adequate attitude
to deal with reality.

60

The base of a community
is the knowledge of the Tao.
This implies that we know
the eternal and impersonal on one side
and on the other side, the personal "I".
The balance of both
is the harmony in the community.
There is no need for ruling or leading
when each individual masters this balance.
Living together is the natural way of being human.
There is no perfect recipe for it
nor any specific rule,
but, by following the natural flow of existence,
we do what is necessary
without sticking to our personal truth.

61

Living in the knowledge of the Tao,
we truly become powerful.
It's not about having power over
something or someone;
it's about being power.
Normally we understand power
as something we have,
but in the Tao, it is what we are.
A truly powerful human being remains
still, receptive and detached.
The more powerful we are,
the more humble we get.
When we understand how little is the personal "I"
and how vast is the impersonal I Amness,
humility is the logical and inevitable consequence.
Humility is trusting the Tao.

62

Everything comes from the Tao,
the Tao is more than everything.
It is the most loved treasure
and the refuge for all in need.
It doesn't matter who you are
or what you have done,
it shares infinite love with everyone.
The Tao abandons nobody
but we can close our hearts and minds
pretending that we don't feel it.
To share the Tao
is the gift of all gifts
the most noble action.

63

Concentrate on the small things
and success will come by itself.
Do without acting, work naturally
and let things happen.
In the time of loss and failure, learn.
In the time of success and winning,
step back and remain serene.
Focus on the simple
and you will manage the complex.
Learn from nature.
She is the guide for real success.
Every work is done by thousands of small steps,
remember this when difficulty arises.
Forget about being special,
that means the others are not.
Forget about being the winner
it requires the others to be losers.
Dreams about greatness
take you away from the present moment.
Living in the Tao is the real success.

64
If the structure of suffering is known,
suffering is not a problem anymore.
If the structure of serenity is known,
suffering vanishes.
This knowledge is impersonal.
It travels from one person
to another throughout time;
the words change but the meaning remains.
Being rooted in the Tao
reveals this knowledge.
All you have to do is focus on it,
the rest will come naturally.

65

Don't try to educate people,
share the non-knowing
and how to enter emptiness.
Thinking that we know the answer,
in a world of constant change,
is the beginning of the "intelligence of ignorance".
Thinking that we don't know the answer,
opens us to the flow of evolution;
it's flexible, humble, gentle and sensitive.
In this way, we can find our own way.
Avoid being vain.
The simple patterns are the most easy to spot.
The simple life is the most easy to live.
When you can see the wonder of life
in one single breath, you see it everywhere.

66

The sea is vast, welcoming all rivers.
The clouds are light or heavy nourishing the earth.
Sometimes the water is liquid,
then vapour or frozen;
but it doesn't matter which form it takes -
it will be always water.
To recognise yourself in one single drop of water
is humility and power at the same time.
When the egocentric mind
tries to tell stories
about what should be and what should not be,
remember the drop of water,
remember who you really are.
If you want to do good or even change the world,
remember the drop;
do it in the humility of the water

67

The Tao is rational and irrational,
logical and non-logical.
Thoughts stay on the surface.
Only when the Tao is practiced,
is the understanding completely present
in every cell of the body.
In the practice of the Tao
we realise four fundamental aspects:
simplicity, patience, humility and compassion.
Being simple in action and thought,
we understand the inner structure of nature.
Being patient with all living things,
we are in harmony with the world.
Being humble we know
that everything is connected.
Being compassionate with ourselves,
we are compassionate with all existence.

68

One thing is doing the best you can
but it is something completely different
trying to be the best.
The winner-concept
makes us all losers.
The glorification of being the number one
eliminates the essence of playing.
Competition itself creates separation.
Our wins will always be the losses of others.
Young minds are still in the essence of playing,
they play for playing.
When the heart is full and the mind at peace,
the wish to be the best vanishes.
Evolution is about playing and making mistakes
and not a competition to figure out who is the best.

69

The ego is the natural function of the mind.
In this way we become conscious about ourselves
and therefore about the world.
Using it in this way, it is the most beautiful tool.
Tools always depend on how we use them.
If we use them in their natural way,
beauty and harmony are the result;
but, use them in the wrong way,
or for the wrong purpose, insanity will be the result.
The common misunderstanding
is to believe that we are the ego
and that the ego is in charge of "its" life;
the ego on one side
and all the rest on the other side.
This belief system
is the disease and the drama of humanity.
By practicing the Tao we will heal this disease.

70

The words and actions are simple;
too simple for the thinking mind.
The intellect likes to grasp it
but you never can hold the Tao.
The Tao is older than the world,
do you really believe that it can be yours?
Finding the Tao in your heart
you will find it in the world.

71

Wisdom is to know your degree of ignorance.
Pretending that you know leads to imbalance.
First you have to know how little you know,
then true knowledge will come.
Non-knowing is freedom from mental slavery.
When you are open to what is,
you are ready to see the wonder.
But when you are full of knowledge,
then you see only
your limitation or your wishful thinking.
Being empty is the secret of the Tao.

72

When you lose the awareness
of the present moment,
you lose contact with yourself.
Not knowing who you are
will push you forward
to follow someone or something.
It could be a religion, some kind of leadership,
the latest fashion or simply following authority.
This creates the vicious circle of external needs.
The person who lives in self-knowledge
will stay calm and at peace.
One has no need to interfere
in the business of people, nor to show up
and present yourself as somebody who knows.

73

Action of non-action.
It's not a passive way at all.
It's the effortlessly action
in alignment with the ebb and flow of life.
It's the doing without the sense of "I do".
It is the action without a condition
nor projection to the outcome.
It is goodness without the wish for a reward;
the doing without trying.
When we lose it,
we are lost in the mind.
Confusion and resistance will be our shadow.
In the action of non-action we are
at one with the Tao.
All separations are unified.

74

Nothing exists as a solid and determinate thing.
All is in constant movement.
There is nothing to hold on to.
We live in the illusion of a world of solid things,
but it exists only as a delusion in our minds.
We believe in solid things,
in our insatiable need for control.
We want to have a fixed reality,
it gives us the feeling of security
and the illusion of non-death.
Everything is dying now,
everything is reborn now.
If you aren't afraid of dying,
there is nothing you can lose.

75

When you live attached to things
you will never have enough.
In the constant search for the new and the better,
your heart becomes poisoned
with wishful thinking.
When the heart is full and the mind is empty,
you can act to benefit all existence,
without the need for a reward.
It's all about trust.
Trust in yourself.
Trust in the heart.
Trust in the flow of life.
Trust in the Tao.

76

Life is the dance of opposites
in the rhythm of adversity and harmony.
If we dance gentle and flexible
we are a disciple of life.
If we dance hard and inflexible
we are a disciple of death.
If the dancer becomes the dance
we learn how to be a disciple of life.

77

The Tao is the perfect balance.
Excess, control, fear, extremes and egoism
go against the Tao.
But nothing can go for long against it;
the balance will always go with the Tao.
Living in that consciousness
is the key to overcoming
all hindrances and obstacles.

78

The real truth goes beyond all definitions,
it has no name.
There is nothing to defend.
There is nothing to fight for.
This inner state is light in the darkness.
This light shines on the way of the Tao.
It's pure perfection.

79

Failure is an opportunity.
Blame does not exist in the real world,
it is just an illusion of the mind.
Serenity is the consequence of this understanding.

80

There is nothing more than the Tao.
Oneness is its nature.
Seeing everything as one
is awakened consciousness.
Seeing the oneness in the world,
heals all conflicts.
Seeing the oneness in others,
is love.
Feeling oneness in your heart,
is serenity.
Being serene is fulfilment.
Fulfilment is the purpose of life.

81
The Tao is all there is and more;
you are the Tao.
Living in this knowledge is
being in Love with Life.

Thank you for reading this book. I hope that it serves you. If you want to visit my web page, you will find more information about my work.

Have a great day

www.karstenramser.net[1]

If the book was useful for you, please remember to leave a review for the book at your favorite retailer.

---

1.   http://www.karstenramser.net/

THE TAO OF THE 21ST CENTURY

A note about the book.

The right book comes at the right time, probably we all know this experience. Sometimes this kind of book suddenly enters our lives; other times it stays for years on the bookshelf and maybe we have read it already but without comprehending its essence.

There is the saying that "the master comes when the disciple is ready". The same happens with special books; they come to us when we are ready for them.

For me, the Tao Te Ching is one of these books.

Some 30 years ago I heard for the first time about the Tao and from then on it has crossed my path sometimes; I even had a copy of the Tao Te Ching in my library. But, it sounded a little old fashioned, using themes like: the superior and inferior man; governing people; the master does this, the master does that and so on.

At the end of 2016, I read it again and was able to look beyond the appearance seeing the deep beauty of this amazing book and it marked a turning point in my life.

It is for this reason that I wrote the Tao of the 21st century.

Historical background

2500 years ago, Lao-Tse wrote the Tao Te Ching. It is the most important work written about the Tao.

The social-cultural background of the book was the Warring States period (around 500BC), a time of external turmoil, chaos and war. It was also the time when the foundation of the Chinese philosophy flourished, giving birth to the two main philosophies of China: Taoism and Confucianism. Simultaneously in Europe the Greek philosophies emerged and the impact is similar.

The Tao influenced Chinese culture in a similar manner to which Greek philosophy influenced European culture.

Very little is known about the author. A lot of legends exist around Lao-Tse but nothing historical. There are no teachings, no testimonies; he is somehow like the book itself; ungraspable - like smoke in the air. He wrote the Tao Te Ching and disappeared.

What we do know, is that the Tao Te Ching is one of the most influential books ever written and after the Bible, it is the most translated book of all time. Thousands of interpretations and commentaries exist and the Tao Te Ching is an essential part of Chinese culture.

The Tao Te Ching also gives birth to Taoism, the religious and institutional expression of the Tao. The Tao Te Ching is also an essential part of Confucianism and of many spiritual traditions and philosophical schools in China.

In the 20th century, China entered a very materialistic time. First there was the Nationalist Period, which embraced western way of thinking, rejecting ancient traditions and later on, with communism and the cultural revolution, this rejection increased dramatically.

In the west the Tao was known in the 20th century when oriental philosophies where introduced, but never became as popular as Buddhism or Hinduism.

THE TAO OF THE 21ST CENTURY

Nowadays, many people have heard of the Tao, but very few know what it is really about.

Thanks to:

Maribel Rosado for her being and patience, without her this book would not have been written.

Michael, my brother, his death was a profound inspiration to deepen the need to share the Selfknowledge. Lali Abad for her smiles, good vibrations and proofreading, she is always present when a friend is needed. Jane Williams for her help to put the words together. Manuel Ollero for given the last touch. Delek she is always present in a kind way. Lao Tse and all the people which have worked with the Tao.

About the author:

Karsten Ramser is a painter, sculptor, video-maker, writer, therapist and coach of consciousness.

His work transmit that conscious development is a creative process which transcends the personal I. Once we understand that we are not only our personal story, we can leave behind mental and emotional slavery, entering the vast field of creative consciousness.

This field is the inspiration and centre of his writings and his artwork.

Conscious development and real art, are one process.

Karsten Ramser works with The Art of Consciousness which in a practical way to discover our most inner nature.

"Everybody can wake up, the only thing we need is the inner thirst for it. Of course it is not easy, but the path is there".

Conscious Art is his individual expression of being connected with the field of creative consciousness.

He believe that Consciousness is not personal and for this he shares the beauty and the how to integrate it in our life's as an living experience.

"Life is the ultimate artwork, our job is to discover it, and the how we do this is, the Art of Consciousness".

I invite you to explore and discover my other artworks:

<u>CONSCIOUS ART</u>[1]
<u>PAINTING</u>[2]
<u>SCULPTURE</u>[3]
<u>PHOTOPAINTING</u>[4]
<u>MOTION</u>[5]
More information and contact:
<u>www.karstenramser.net</u>[6]
<u>Facebook</u>[7]
<u>Instagram</u>[8]
<u>@ Contact @</u>[9]
For All

---

1. **https://www.karstenramser.net/conscius-art**

2. https://www.karstenramser.net/gewahrsein-painting-english

3. https://www.karstenramser.net/becoming-sculptures

4. https://www.karstenramser.net/photo-painting

5. https://www.karstenramser.net/motion

6. http://www.karstenramser.net/

7. http://www.facebook.com/karsten.ramser

8. https://www.instagram.com/karstenramser/

9. http://www.karstenramser.net/contact

Contents